About the author

A portion of the proceeds from this book will be donated to the National Center of Missing and Exploited Children (NcMEC), a private, non-profit 501(c)(3) whose mission is "to help find missing children, reduce child sexual exploitation, and prevent child victimization." Despite the crass humor and aggressive language written on the following pages, the soul of this book belongs to children, so it only felt right to give back to an organization that never stops looking for them.

Alexandra Taylor

PARENTING THINGS:
A THIRD PARTY OBSERVATION

Vanguard Press

VANGUARD PAPERBACK

© Copyright 2024
Alexandra Taylor

The right of Alexandra Taylor to be identified as author
of this work has been asserted by them in accordance with the
Copyright, Designs and Patents Act 1988.

All Rights Reserved

No reproduction, copy or transmission of this publication
may be made without written permission.
No paragraph of this publication may be reproduced,
copied or transmitted save with the written permission of the publisher,
or in accordance with the provisions
of the Copyright Act 1956 (as amended).

Any person who commits any unauthorised act in relation to this publication
may be liable to criminal prosecution and civil claims for damages.

A CIP catalogue record for this title is available from the British Library.

ISBN 978-1-80016-969-2

This is a work of fiction. Names, characters, businesses, places, events and
incidents are either the products of the author's imagination or used in a
fictitious manner. Any resemblance to actual persons, living or dead, or actual
events is purely coincidental.

Vanguard Press is an imprint of
Pegasus Elliot Mackenzie Publishers Ltd.
www.pegasuspublishers.com

First Published in 2024

Vanguard Press
Sheraton House Castle Park
Cambridge England

Printed & Bound in Great Britain

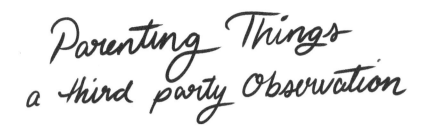

Parenting Things
a third party Observation

Written by: Alexandra Taylor
Illustrated by: Mattea Valdovinos
Editor: Brittany Hart
Handwriting by: My mom, Shawn Taylor

Dedications:
I dedicate this book to all the mothers, mother-figures and helping hands (dads, aunts & uncles, grandparents, teachers, friends, day-care providers, babysitters, nannies, etc); when it comes to raising a child in this current nightmare of a world, you all seem to make life a little easier to navigate and conquer.
And most importantly – the biggest shout out of all goes to Shawn Taylor – I'm so happy I chose you as my mommy. I love you.

Acknowledgements:
To Mike: You might not understand me all the time, but you support me no matter what I set out to do. Thank you for loving me. I love you.

Donation:
A portion of the proceeds from this book will be donated to the National Center of Missing and Exploited Children (NcMEC), a private, non-profit 501(c)(3) whose mission is "to help find missing children, reduce child sexual exploitation, and prevent child victimization."

Despite the crass humor and aggressive language written on the following pages, the soul of this book belongs to children, so it only felt right to give back to an organization that that never stops looking for them.

Opinions about parenting from someone who has never fucking done it

BABYSITTERS ARE CRITICAL SO LIVING NEAR PARENTS MEANS FREE CHILDCARE.

IF YOU NEED A MINUTE TO REST, PUT ON SOME DISNEY MOVIES. WHILE THEY ARE A BLESSING IN DISGUISE, THEY ARE ALSO A CURSE AS YOUR CHILD WILL ASK FOR THE MOVIES TO BE PLAYED OVER & OVER & OVER & OVER...

KNOW THAT FOUR-YEAR-OLD KIDDIES ARE ALWAYS RIGHT;
> THEY DON'T CARE ABOUT LOGIC OR REASON.

IGNORING A CHILD DOES NOT MEAN THAT THEY WILL BECOME EXHAUSTED OF ASKING THE SAME QUESTION - IF ANYTHING, IT WILL GIVE THEM FUEL TO BEGIN TUGGING HARDER & SHOUTING LOUDER UNTIL THEY FEEL THAT THEY HAVE BEEN APPROPRIATELY RESPONDED TO.
   (OR THEY GET WHAT THEY WANT.)

DON'T CUNT PUNT A KID —
 IT'S USUALLY NOT WELL RECEIVED BY OTHERS.

GIBBERISH IS THE UNIVERSAL LANGUAGE OF TODDLERS. ALWAYS NOD YOUR HEAD IN AGREEMENT EVEN IF YOU HAVE NO GODDAMN IDEA WHAT THEY ARE SAYING.

YOUR CHILD IS NOT THAT SPECIAL.

TREAT CHILDREN LIKE YOUR BLACKED OUT BEST FRIEND
THEY'RE GOING TO ANNOY THE SHIT OUT OF YOU
BUT YOU LOVE THOSE MOTHERFUCKERS.

IF YOUR HOUSE IS QUIET THEN SOME SERIOUSLY MISCHIEVOUS SHIT IS GOING ON.

IF YOUR CHILD HAS A DIAPER FILLED WITH PISS OR SHIT, YOU DON'T NEED TO ASK FOR THEIR CONSENT TO CHANGE IT. DO YOU REMEMBER YOUR PARENTS CHANGING YOUR DIAPERS? (NEWSFLASH DIPSHIT, YOU PROBABLY DON'T REMEMBER BECAUSE YOU WERE A FUCKING BABY, NOT BECAUSE YOU WERE BILL COSBY'D).

I think you need to change their diaper...

But they didn't verbally say I could so I would be basically molesting them!

IF YOU'RE ON A PLANE WITH A BABY:
EXPECT SHIT TO GET TURBULENT.

* IN THE EVENT OF A SCREAMER, REMEMBER TO FILL YOUR COCKTAIL GLASS FIRST BEFORE ASSISTING OTHERS.

this is why our babies can't fly yet

WHILE IT TAKES A VILLAGE TO RAISE A CHILD, SOMETIMES, THE VILLAGE NEEDS TO BACK-THE-FUCK-UP AND LET THE PARENT BE THE PARENT.

STOP FUCKING ASKING A WOMAN WHEN
"SHE'S PLANNING ON HAVEING KIDS"
A WOMAN CAN STILL FEEL FULFILLED IN LIFE,
EVEN IF HER WOMB IS CURRENTLY UNOCCUPIED

IF YOUR KID IS IN THE STAGE WHERE THEY ARE CONSTANTLY SCREAMING, PLEASE DON'T FUCKING BRING THEM TO A RESTAURANT
— YOU'RE RUINING IT FOR EVERYONE ELSE.

STOP BRINGING BABIES TO THE MOVIE THEATRES! NOTHING ELSE NEEDS TO BE SAID.

IF YOUR CHILD LIKES TO INTENTIONALLY HURT ANIMALS, THEN YOU NEED TO KNOW:

A. YOU HAVE A DAHMER-LIKE PROBLEM ON YOUR HANDS OR
B. YOUR KID IS AN ASSHOLE AND IT'S YOUR FAULT FOR NOT CORRECTING THIS BEHAVIOR.

This page is specifically dedicated to Karen Kilgariff & Georgia Hardstark

Your child does not need their own Instagram account;

Hotbabee300

0 likes

PEOPLE ARE GOING TO SWEAR WHETHER OR NOT YOUR BABY IS AROUND. GET OVER IT. EXCUSE ME, I MEANT TO SAY, GET THE FUCK OVER IT.

CHILDREN AREN'T BORN RACIST, HOMOPHOBIC, OR MEAN. TEACH THEM HOW TO LOVE AND RESPECT OTHERS.

IF YOU'RE A VEGAN, THAT'S COOL AND ALL

* BUT THERE'S NO NEED TO FORCE YOUR VEGAN LIFESTYLE ON YOUR KID. YOUR CHILD CAN STILL BE A DECENT HUMAN BEING AND EAT MEAT. LET THE FRUIT OF YOUR LOINS MAKE THEIR OWN FOOD CHOICES WHEN THEY CAN COMPREHEND COMPLEX DIETARY, ENVIRONMENTAL, SOCIETAL, AND ANIMAL IMPACTS.

* UNLESS YOU'RE ONE OF THOSE VEGANS THAT LETS EVERYONE KNOW THAT YOU'RE A VEGAN. THEN FUCK YOU, YOU ANNOYING SOY CURD.

GIRLS CAN WEAR BLUE AND PLAY WITH TOY TRUCKS. BOYS CAN HAVE LONG HAIR AND PLAY WITH BARBIE DOLLS. ALL THAT MATTERS IS THAT THEY ARE HAPPY AND LOVED

IT'S CREEPY WHEN YOU MAKE YOUR CHILD'S OUTFIT MATCH YOUR OWN.

FOR THE LOVE OF GOD / ALLAH
         (INSERT DEITY CHOICE HERE)
PLEASE VACCINATE YOUR CHILDREN.

> Hey Janice, I have a joke for you. Why was the unvaccinated 3yr old crying? Because they were having a mid-life crisis! But seriously vaccinate your fucking kid.

A PREGNANT WOMAN IS ALLOWED TO HAVE A DRINK
(REPEATING THIS — SINGULAR)
RANDOM STRANGERS WHO HAVE A RUNNING COMMENTARY ABOUT THIS SHOULD KNOW THAT
THEIR INPUT IS NOT FUCKING WELCOMED.

MEN - GET IT THROUGH YOUR HEADS:
"WE" ARE NOT PREGNANT.

YOUR BABY MAMMA IS THE ONE GROWING A PARASITE IN HER UTERUS FOR 9 MONTHS AND PUSHING THAT THING(S) OUT. "YOU" NEED TO CHECK YOURSELF.

A LITTLE DAB OF RUM IN A TEETHING BABY'S MOUTH NEVER HURT ANYONE.

FOR GOD'S SAKE, DON'T HOVER! YOUR CHILD WILL NEVER LEARN HOW TO EXPLORE, BE INDEPENDENT, OR GROW IF YOU DON'T LET THEM TRY (AND FAIL). RESPECT HOW THEY LEARN.

(WARNING: IT MIGHT BE DIFFERENT THAN YOUR STYLE!) BY GIVING THEM SPACE, THEY'LL THANK YOU LATER ON.

IF THERE IS A STANDING PREGNANT WOMAN NEAR YOU, THE RIGHT THING TO DO IS OFFER UP YOUR SEAT LIKE A GODDAMN CIVILIZED HUMAN BEING

DO NOT, I REPEAT, DO NOT FUCKING TOUCH A PREGNANT PERSON'S BELLY WITHOUT ASKING. EVER.

THERE IS NEVER A NEED TO COMMENT ON HOW FAT OR SKINNY A PREGNANT WOMAN LOOKS.
JESUS CHRIST - DO WOMEN EVER GET A BREAK?

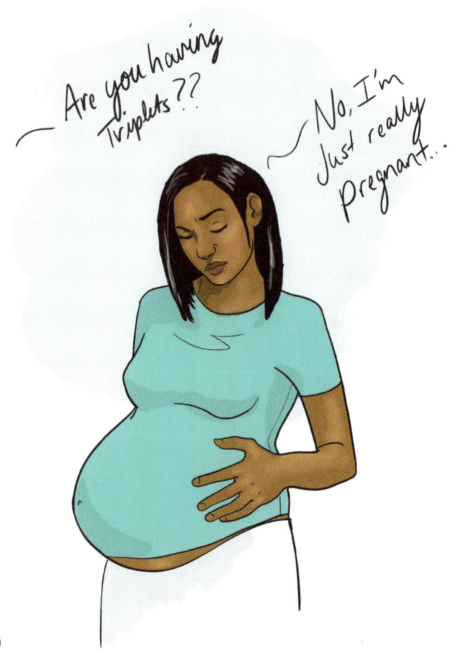

AND FOR GOD'S SAKE, NEVER ASK A WOMAN IF SHE'S "PREGGERS".

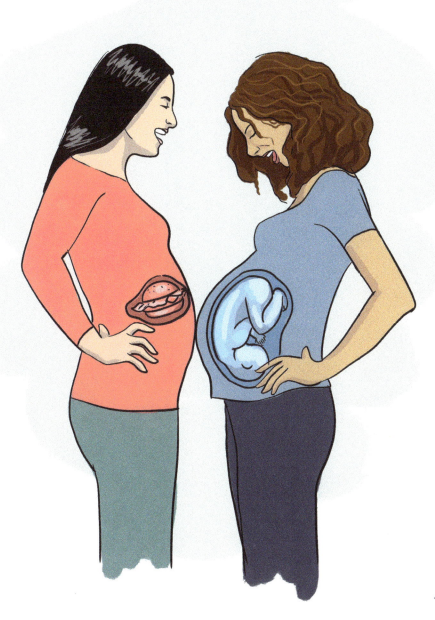

AND IF SOMEONE IS CONSTANTLY BULLYING OR HARASSING YOUR CHILD AND YOUR CHILD CANNOT APPROPRIATELY DEFEND THEMSELVES, YOU HAVE EVERY RIGHT TO FUCK UP THAT P.O.S.* (PIECE OF SHIT) AND ALSO EVISCERATE THEIR PARENT(S).

*P.O.S. CAN ALSO INCLUDE (BUT NOT LIMITED TO) TEACHERS, COACHES, AND EVEN FAMILY MEMBERS.

HAVING A DOG IS NOTHING LIKE HAVING A BABY. I DON'T HAVE EITHER, BUT I GUARANTEE THAT ONE IS A LITTLE BIT MORE TIME CONSUMING.

A CHILD IS NOT A FASHION ACCESSORY.

I'M JUST GOING TO SAY IT - NOT EVERY BABY IS CUTE. SOME BABIES ARE JUST FUCKING UGLY. I MEAN, YOUR BABY IS GORGEOUS, OBVIOUSLY. IT'S "OTHER" PEOPLE'S BABIES THAT ARE FUGLY.

SHAKING A BABY IS NO BUENO

Acceptable items to shake

1. Salt shakers

2. Polaroids

3. Hands

4. Cocktails

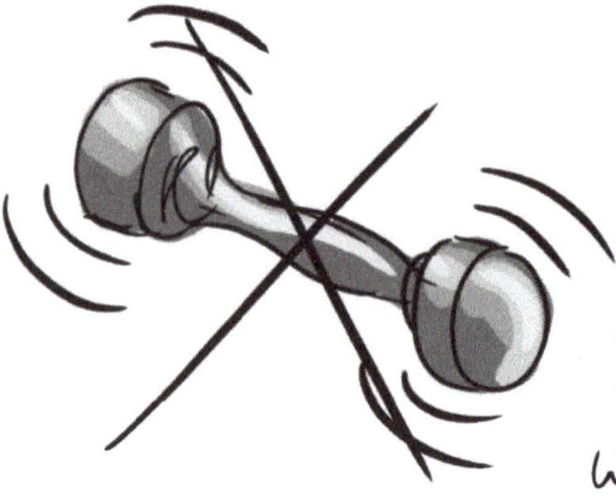

shake weights will never be accepted

BABY BJORNS ARE EXCLUSIVELY RESERVED FOR BABIES AND NOT YOUR PUPPY. IF YOU HAVE SOMETHING OTHER THAN A BABY IN A BABY BJORN, THAT'S JUST STRAIGHT UP NOT OKAY.

BOTTLE OR BOOB.
FEED YOUR BABY HOWEVER YOU SEE FIT

JUST BECAUSE ALL OF YOUR FRIENDS ARE HAVING KIDS DOESN'T MEAN YOU HAVE TO. SUCCUMBING TO PEER PRESSURE IS NEVER A GOOD IDEA — WHETHER IT'S A TEQUILA SHOT OR HAVING A BABY.
IF YOU'RE NOT READY TO BECOME A PARENT, THEN DON'T! EVERYONE IS READY AT THEIR OWN PACE.

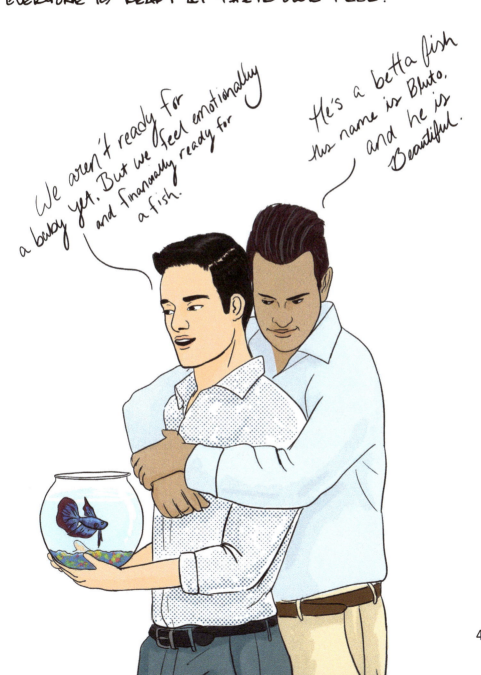

THAT BEING SAID,
THERE IS NEVER A PERFECT TIME TO HAVE A KID.

Love the shit out of that little shit!

A young woman holds her newborn son and looks at him lovingly. Softly she sings to him:

"I'll love you forever
I'll like you for always
As long as I'm living
My baby you'll be"

I'm sure many of you remember that heartwarming story. My mom used to read it to me as a child. Well, news flash fuckers, this book isn't anything like that.

Parenting Things is an earnest examination about the trials, taboos, and exhaustion that comes with parenting*.

*from someone who has never fucking done it.

Printed in the USA
CPSIA information can be obtained
at www.ICGtesting.com
LVHW071150240824
789145LV00010B/73